T0382371

British Society for International Understanding

BRITISH SURVEY HANDBOOKS
General Editor: JOHN EPPSTEIN

V

DENMARK

CAMBRIDGE
UNIVERSITY PRESS

University Printing House, Cambridge CB2 8BS, United Kingdom

Cambridge University Press is part of the University of Cambridge.

It furthers the University's mission by disseminating knowledge in the pursuit of
education, learning and research at the highest international levels of excellence.

www.cambridge.org
Information on this title: www.cambridge.org/9781107426153

© Cambridge University Press 1945

First published 1945
First paperback edition 2014

A catalogue record for this publication is available from the British Library

ISBN 978-1-107-42615-3 Paperback

Additional resources for this publication at www.cambridge.org/9781107426153

BRITISH SURVEY HANDBOOKS

DENMARK

CAMBRIDGE
AT THE UNIVERSITY PRESS
1945

NOTE

The object of the series of British Survey Handbooks is to give essential information about the history, economic life, conditions and outlook of the various nations of Europe, and of the effects of the war upon them.

This handbook has been compiled by the British Society for International Understanding in collaboration with the Danish Council Information Office. It is the joint work of Mr Sten Gudme, who has contributed the two chapters on Denmark under the German occupation, Mr Blytgen Petersen, Mr Anker Svart and Miss Kathleen Gibberd.

An appendix gives practical guidance upon municipal government, social legislation and other matters of interest to those whose duties may take them to Denmark during or after its liberation.

JOHN EPPSTEIN
Editor

April 1945

CONTENTS

CONTENTS

DENMARK

CHAPTER I

AN OUTLINE OF DANISH HISTORY

THE VIKINGS. Although Denmark is one of the
oldest Kingdoms of Europe, there is little authentic
history of events in the country before the ninth
century. Tradition and legend, however, are
abundant, and some of these old stories are
highly fanciful—as, for instance, one which pictures Noah disembarking from the Ark on the coast
of Jutland. Others, preserved in sagas, or told by
early chroniclers, corroborate one another in the
general presentation of heroic and often blood-
thirsty chieftains (Vikings) warring among themselves, or, in search of 'living-room' and adventure,
raiding the coasts and river channels of other
countries. Massacres were not at all uncommon,
and the story of Hamlet as recorded by a Danish
chronicler ends in a far larger number of deaths
than does the version which appears to have been
used by Shakespeare; the climax is, in fact, the
trapping of a banqueting party who are all burnt
to death by the avenging Prince. The people of
to-day are the descendants of these extravagant
warriors, and their history shows a gradual development from the role of a people feared by their
neighbours to that of the most pacific country
in Europe.

Denmark adopted Christianity later than other

northern countries of Europe. While Charlemagne was baptizing by force the peoples whom he had conquered, the Danes continued to be pagans. During the latter half of the eighth century there begin to be increasing references to the Danes in the annals of other European nations. They were feared throughout northern Europe where, as time went on, they appeared in increasing numbers as formidable raiders who sailed up the estuaries of rivers and made new homes for themselves at the point of the sword. As a result a new phrase was temporarily added to the Anglo-Saxon Litany: 'From the fury of the Danes, deliver us, Oh Lord.'

In England a great part of the country fell into their hands, and the invaders were only checked by the leadership and strategy of King Alfred the Great who won a decisive victory in 878. The Danes then sued for peace, and thirty of their leading men came to Alfred to be baptized. Under the ensuing agreement the Danes were confined within a prescribed region on the east coast—the Danelaw—and there they made permanent settlement.

Rather more than a hundred years later, however, another English King, Ethelred the Unready, did not fare so well. He tried to buy off the Danes with money raised especially for this purpose (Danegeld), and finally, by the senseless massacre of a number of Danes, including the sister of the Danish King, he provoked King Sweyn of Denmark into an avenging mission which resulted in the sacking and pillaging of East Anglia and southern England. Defeated and his forces routed, Ethelred was obliged to flee to Normandy.

CANUTE THE GREAT. Sweyn died before he could enjoy his triumphs and his young son Canute became King of England, while his eldest son Harold succeeded to the throne of Denmark. By marrying Ethelred's widow, Canute the Great (as he was afterwards called) united the two royal families of England and Denmark, and by a conciliatory policy towards the English and a refusal to favour the Danes, he won the approbation of the English people. Later, Canute succeeded to the Danish throne, and a successful expedition to Norway ended by his being acclaimed King of that country also. Thus for a short time England, Denmark and Norway were united under one King. Danish rule over England ended shortly after Canute's death when the throne reverted to the English line of Kings.

One result of the temporary union of Denmark and England was that a number of English monks went to found monasteries in Denmark, thus helping to consolidate the original missionary work of Ansgar, a learned and pious monk who had introduced Christianity into the country about the year 826. But despite the growing influence of the new religion the eleventh and twelfth centuries were a period of great internal disturbance, and it was only when Valdemar gained the undisputed sovereignty of Denmark in 1157, after the violent deaths of his rivals, that better days set in.

DENMARK UNDER THE VALDEMARS. Under Valdemar I, Canute IV and Valdemar II, the country enjoyed a hundred years of prosperity. The King's power was consolidated through conquests in the

Baltic states during wars with the Wends who used to raid the provinces in the south of Sweden, then under the Danish crown. In the south, the Danish frontier was pushed as far as the Elbe. Denmark was thus for a time a great power.

Absalon, Bishop of Roskilde and Archbishop of Lund, Denmark's first great statesman (1128–1201), was both a spiritual and military leader at this time. Having studied at the University of Paris himself, he encouraged his countrymen to study law and theology there, thereby strengthening the cultural bonds between the west of Europe and the north. The clergy acquired power and wealth through many great gifts and bequests, and new monasteries as well as churches sprang up, many of which are still standing. It was also the beginning of the age of chivalry in Denmark. The feudal system had not yet developed, and the nobility, though of no mean influence, served the King rather as officials than as feudal lords. Many of the best-known Danish folk songs date from this time of the Valdemars. Written anonymously, they were passed on from mouth to mouth and were sung as accompaniments to dances in the Danish castles. It was during this period, also, that Saxo Grammaticus was persuaded by Absalon to write his famous chronicles of early Danish history.

Danish horses were much in demand at this time, especially in England and Germany. Another source of wealth was the great herring fisheries on the coast of Skaane. Here the fish were so numerous that they could be scooped up with the bare hands.

THE POWER OF THE NOBILITY. Internal dissensions broke out again after the death of Valdemar II in 1241 and, in fact, Denmark was the scene of almost uninterrupted strife for the next three hundred years. Apart from trouble with her neighbours and her acquired territories there was a long drawn-out struggle between the King and the Church and also between the King and the nobility. At the beginning of the period three sovereigns met their death by assassination, and during the whole time hardly any held the throne in safety and confidence. A few, like King Valdemar IV and his daughter Margaret, were able to bring benefits to the country. The real power in the land was the nobility, and eventually the Crown became subservient to the Council of State, consisting of the nobility and the chief clergy. It was this Council which appointed each new sovereign. At the end of the sixteenth century Denmark was ruled by an aristocracy. The power of the nobility had been reinforced by the Reformation, for although the nobles had at first resisted the religious change, the final result was the exclusion of the bishops from the Council of State, leaving it a lay assembly. In the meantime the condition of the peasants had deteriorated. Many of them had lost their independence to become tenants or mere serfs and they bore the chief burden of taxation.

WARS WITH SWEDEN. Under Christian IV (1588–1648), the most popular of Danish Kings, partly on account of the engaging simplicity of his personality, but chiefly for his great bravery in battle and devotion to his country, the

Council of State, although outwardly as strong as
ever, was beginning to lose its prestige. The
national assemblies which were summoned for the
purpose of approving legislation voiced widespread
criticism, but it was the disastrous wars with
Sweden in the reign of this King and more especially in that of his successor, Frederick III, which
finally left the Council of State entirely discredited.
The attempt of the Swedes to conquer Denmark
brought King and people more closely together,
and when the enemy besieged Copenhagen the
King led the citizens in preparing the defences and
personally took part in sorties against the besiegers.
The conflict ended with a Danish victory at
Nyborg at the end of 1659 and the death of the
Swedish King at the beginning of the following
year.

ABSOLUTE MONARCHY. A few months later representatives of all classes of the people, except the
peasants, were summoned to a meeting in Copenhagen to furnish money for the payment of the
war debt, for the maintenance of the army and for
the expenses of the Court. The clergy and townspeople were united in a demand for a just sharing
of the burden, but the nobility, who had hitherto
been exempt from taxation, stubbornly refused to
bear a tax on their consumption of food. As a
result of this, the other sections of the community
offered Denmark to the King as a hereditary
Kingdom, similar to the existing Kingdoms of
Sweden, England, France and Spain. The Council
of State declared that the deputies of the people
and of the clergy had no right to make this offer

and refused at first to countenance it. The King, however, finally took his stand against the nobles and was ready to be proclaimed a hereditary monarch by the townspeople and clergy alone, whereupon the Council was obliged to comply (1660). Thus the long period of aristocratic rule ended and was replaced by an absolute monarchy. Having asserted themselves against the nobles, the deputies of the church and towns did not, however, form themselves into a regular assembly. They did not, in fact, meet again for two hundred years.

Nevertheless, the King's counsellors were henceforth drawn largely from the new middle class. One of the first burghers to rise to this high position was Griffenfeld, the son of a wine merchant. Under his able statesmanship the finances of the country were reorganized and foreign trade developed. East and West Indies trading companies received concessions and another company received the monopoly of trade and fishing in Greenland. Foreign capital was given the opportunity to build factories, and the merchant fleet was doubled in the space of two years. Eventually Griffenfeld overreached himself and his intrigues resulted in his imprisonment.

HUMANITARIANISM AND NEUTRALITY. In the meantime, Denmark continued to be involved in wars with her neighbours, resulting in an increasing burden of taxation on her people. The new middle class produced landed proprietors who were as anxious to avoid taxation and to exact forced labour from the peasants as had been the old nobility. In 1733 a measure was introduced which made every farmer's son from his fourteenth to his thirty-sixth year liable either to military service or to work on the land. However, as the eighteenth century advanced, Denmark took a new turn both in foreign relations and in internal affairs. To other countries she adopted an attitude of neutrality which has ever since remained the keynote of her foreign policy. At home the lot of the peasants was finally improved by the abolition of the *Stavnsbaand* in 1788 and the gradual establishment of a free peasantry. The same spirit which revolutionized the lot of the peasants inspired the decision to end the slave trade in the Danish West Indies in 1792. Denmark was the first country to take this step and Britain was the first to follow her example. Another sign of the times was the establishment of the freedom of the press and the provision of free schools. By the end of the eighteenth century Denmark was one of the most liberal countries in Europe: it was also, through its seafaring trade, one of the most prosperous.

WARS WITH ENGLAND. Meanwhile, the Napoleonic wars kept the Western powers occupied; but the Danes, if they wished to sail the seas at all, could not escape being involved. The Danish Government started to convoy Danish merchantmen as a countermeasure against British inspection of neutral vessels, and the whole matter assumed very serious proportions. At this juncture, Russia, who was interested in obstructing Britain, suggested an alliance with Denmark, under the terms of which the partners were to defend their neutrality. In this difficult situation for a small state, Denmark chose not to offend Russia, with the inevitable result that on April 2, 1801, Admirals Parker and Nelson appeared off Copenhagen with a powerful British fleet. The Danes fought bravely, but the British gained the day, and Denmark had to sign harsh peace terms.

A few years later, Denmark's determination to remain neutral led to a second armed conflict with Britain. Fearing that Napoleon might demand the use of the Danish navy—a demand that so small a country would be powerless to resist—the British Government offered Denmark an alliance on condition that the fleet was handed over to Britain, to be returned intact after the war. The Danish Crown Prince Regent (later Frederick VI) indignantly refused this suggestion and hostilities followed. The British landed in Zealand, besieged the capital and, after a long and violent bombardment which laid parts of Copenhagen in ruins, the Danes were forced to surrender. In a fit of anger King Frederick VI ranged himself on the side of Napoleon and later signed a treaty of mutual assistance with France. Denmark's consequent participation in the Napoleonic wars was costly. When the Danish Government signed the Peace of Kiel in 1814, the long-standing union with Norway had been broken and that country was transferred to Swedish rule. Denmark itself was impoverished by the war and the stagnation of trade.

LIMITED MONARCHY. This state of affairs produced criticism of the absolute monarchy and, following the impetus of the French Revolution, there was a general demand for a more democratic

form of government. In response to this the King
instituted four Assemblies, in different parts of the
country. Their function was to 'provide the King
and his successors with the full knowledge of everything that could contribute to the welfare of his
dear and faithful subjects'. In other words, they
could discuss and advise, but they had no authority.
Moreover, they met in private and were not the
freely elected representatives of the people. In the
short reign of the next King, Christian VIII, the
movement for a new Constitution, sponsored by
the Liberal party, gathered momentum and it
gained strength from widespread resentment of
restrictions on the freedom of the press. Christian
VIII resisted the popular will over the Constitution question, but introduced reforms on his own
account. These included a reorganization of the
army, the introduction of a national budget and,
most important of all, the institution of local self-
government for the towns and countryside. This
was a time of important developments for Denmark, not the least of which was the founding of
the first Folk High School[1] by Grundtvig. It was
also a time when the Scandinavian states seemed
to have become aware of their common interests
and racial bond. This growing sentiment was both
expressed and stimulated by the poems of Öhlen-
schläger. But the bloodless revolution which gave
Denmark the much desired new Constitution and
changed the absolute power of the King into a
limited monarchy did not come about until 1849.
Henceforth there was a national parliament, the
Rigsdag, consisting of two houses, the *Folketing* and

[1] See Chapter III.

the *Landsting*. Election to the *Folketing* was open to all, but the *Landsting* was confined to people of property. Restrictions on the personal liberty of citizens were removed.

SCHLESWIG-HOLSTEIN. In the meantime the first Schleswig War (1848–50) broke out between Denmark and Germany, and this had both overshadowed and interfered with the whole question of the Danish Constitution. Schleswig-Holstein lies north of the river Elbe and therefore between Denmark and Germany. From earliest times it had been something of a battleground where Danes and Germans had come into conflict. The two duchies, Schleswig and Holstein, although originally separate, had been brought into an 'indissoluble' Union in 1460 when King Christian I of Denmark was proclaimed Count of Schleswig and Duke of Holstein. But the laws of succession in the duchies were not the same as those which governed succession to the Crown of Denmark, and this made for controversy. With the growth of both German and Danish nationalism the Danes insisted on their claim to Schleswig and the Germans on their right to Holstein, but owing to the Union, each claim amounted to a demand for both duchies. In the first of the two wars (1848–50) which were fought over this question during the nineteenth century the Danes were victorious, and later the Danish King made concessions to the ever-strong local patriotism of the duchies by giving new powers to their representative assemblies. The chief European powers, however, had for some time become interested in the Schleswig-Holstein question as

the ownership of the disputed territories carried
with it certain strategic advantages. A protocol
signed in London in 1852 by the five Great Powers
and also by Sweden and Norway sought both to
recognize the integrity of Denmark and also to
protect German rights in Holstein and Lauenburg
(the small district in the south-east of Holstein).
The result was a vexatious dispute between Prussia
and Austria on the one hand and Denmark on the
other. Later Great Britain proposed a final settlement which would give the two duchies independence under Denmark. Although the Germans
were willing to agree, the Danes were not, for
Schleswig was reckoned an integral part of Denmark and the River Eider (the boundary between
the two duchies) an historic frontier. The firm
stand taken by Denmark had repercussions in
Holstein and in Germany and Austria. Finally, in
1864, Prussian and Austrian forces crossed the
Eider from Holstein into Schleswig and thus invaded what was generally regarded as historic
Danish territory. The Powers intervened and the
situation became further complicated by Austria's
jealousy of Prussia. However, the campaign ended
in 1864 with the defeat of Denmark, and the two
duchies as well as North Schleswig, which was
unquestionably Danish territory, were ceded to
Prussia and Austria. Two years later, as the result
of the war between these two Germanic countries,
the duchies were appropriated by Prussia alone.
Although by the Treaty of Prague which ended
the conflict it was agreed, under pressure from
Napoleon III, that North Schleswig should be
returned to Denmark if a free plebiscite gave a

vote for this reunion, this article was later deleted
from the treaty by Austria and Prussia.

DANISH NEUTRALITY. The crushing defeat of 1864
and the loss of Danish territory have never been
forgotten by the Danes and were partly responsible
for Denmark's neutrality in the two world wars.
But the period which followed the disaster was a
time of great internal development and was inspired by the principle: 'What has been lost without must be won within.' The process of changing
the leasehold tenancies of the farmers into freehold
ownership, which had already begun, was continued, until, with the turn of the century, all but
a fraction of farmland was freehold. While this was
happening a second disaster, of a quite different
kind, threatened the country, for the greatly increasing exports of American and Russian grain
looked like ousting the main export product of
Denmark from the world's markets. To meet this
the Danes radically altered their whole economy
and produced pigs, poultry and butter instead of
corn. At the same time the co-operative societies,
described in a later chapter, became a great feature
in the marketing of produce. In the last few years
of the century there was a measure for providing
State help to start small farms, and Health Insurance
and Old Age Pensions were also introduced.

When war broke out in Europe in 1914 all
parties were in favour of neutrality. There was an
immediate problem when the Germans followed
the British declaration of war with an inquiry as
to whether the Danes were going to lay mines in
Danish seas. The Germans made it clear that they

would do so themselves unless the Danes complied. With memories of 1864 still vivid the Danes had no choice; but the situation became easier when the British Government raised no objection in view of Denmark's difficult situation. Neutrality did not save the country from the effects of the war. Her trade suffered from the submarine warfare of the Germans and from the blockade of the Allies, and there was widespread unemployment. The victory of the Allies, however, brought her the restoration of North Schleswig, which was reunited to Denmark after the plebiscite of 1920.

During the war there were various constitutional changes. The electoral system was reformed, bringing in universal suffrage and some degree of proportional representation. Iceland was given independence under the Danish Crown, but with Denmark retaining charge of foreign relations. Also, against a good deal of opposition, the Government sold the Danish West Indies to the United States.

BETWEEN THE WARS

In the period between the wars Denmark was a staunch supporter of the League of Nations, and under a Social-Democrat Government she adopted a policy of complete disarmament which involved the reduction of the army and navy to a police force and the dismantling of fortifications.

Although drawn into closer union with the other Scandinavian countries during the 1930's, the Danish Government of 1938 refused a proposal for rearmament in co-operation with them. It was anxious not to offend Germany. The German minority numbering some 20,000 in Schleswig was a cause of anxiety, and a secret campaign was being conducted by one Captain Pflugk-Hartung, who used a small corps of so-called newspaper correspondents to infiltrate Nazi sentiments into the Danish press. Although the Danish people as a whole were very anti-German, the authorities turned a blind eye to German intrigues. In 1939, at Germany's request, Denmark and Germany concluded a Non-Aggression Pact. This, however, did not prevent the Germans from invading Denmark the following year.

The conditions of the occupation and the resistance of the Danes are described in another chapter.

CHAPTER II

THE COUNTRY DESCRIBED

A PENINSULA AND ISLANDS. Denmark, a country half the size of Scotland and one of the smallest independent states in the world, consists of a peninsula and many islands in the north of Europe. Jutland, the Danish peninsula, extends abruptly northwards from Germany in the direction of Norway, and the most southern part of Sweden lies immediately to the east of it. In the seas between Jutland and Sweden are the chief Danish islands, so closely placed against each other and the mainland as almost to block the sea passage from north to south, from the Kattegat to the Baltic. A few miles from the Swedish coast is Zealand, the largest and most important island of Denmark, containing the capital, Copenhagen. In normal times Zealand and Sweden are in daily contact by means of the ferry services which cross the Sound from Elsinore and Copenhagen to the Swedish ports of Halsingborg and Malmö. The smaller island of Fünen lies between Zealand and Jutland and is so close to the peninsula that a bridge had been constructed over the Little Belt to connect the two. The main sea route through the islands is by way of the Great Belt which separates Zealand and Fünen.

The total number of Danish islands is about five hundred, but the majority are mere islets and only a hundred are inhabited. They mostly lie in the neighbourhood of Zealand and Fünen; here, for instance, are Laaland, Falster, Moen and Langeland.

Others, including Samsö, Anholt and Lessö, are scattered in the Kattegat, and there are others, of which Fanö is chiefly important, off the west coast of Jutland. Farther away is the rocky island of Bornholm in the Baltic, and in the North Atlantic, north of the Shetlands, are the Faeroe Islands. Greenland, the largest island in the world, lying mostly in the Arctic Circle and near the American Continent, has been a Danish colony from early times.

Since no part of Denmark is many miles from the sea the climate is less subject to extremes than other parts of Europe on the same latitude—central Russia, for instance. The summer is not unlike the English summer, and the winter, although usually accompanied by prolonged periods of frost and moderate snowfalls, is not severe. The sea also brings varying winds and the weather changes swiftly from day to day as in England.

A traveller flying over Jutland and the islands of Denmark would be chiefly impressed by two features: the low level of the whole country and the extraordinary extent to which the land has been put under cultivation. He would also see how land and water interpenetrate one another, for, apart from the many islands, the coastline is frequently indented by fjords, and in the interior of the country, besides the many lakes, a great number of small rivers take a meandering course to the sea.

JUTLAND. The great plain of mid-Europe extends into Denmark, and the whole country is entirely without mountains or even high hills. It would be a mistake, however, to think of the landscape as flat and monotonous. The wild west coast of Jutland, for instance—usually the first view of the country gained by the visitor from Britain—is different from any other part of the country. Beaten by the winds and waves of the North Sea, this is the only inhospitable shore of Denmark. Until recently Esbjerg, the termination of the sea route from Harwich and the home of a large fishing fleet, was the only harbour here, but in the early 1930's two others were constructed at Hirshals and Hvide Sande. Other ports are projected. These developments follow the protection of this coast by breakwaters and an extensive reclamation of the hinterland. The greater part of this bare and desolate coast consists of sand dunes, and until recently the immediate interior was a waste land of sandy heath and bog, broken towards the north by a chain of fjords, and rendered unfertile by the sand which blew in from the dunes. This process of deterioration, however, was checked and some 2000 square miles have been brought under cultivation by the efforts of the Society for the Reclamation of the Moors and by the perseverance of individual farmers. This work was subsidized by the State and the results are seen in the fields of crops, the pastures and young forests, which in the course of seventy years have usurped half the domain of heath, bog and sand.

Eastern Jutland has quite a different landscape and in the south it is not unlike the English countryside. Here are hills, undulating fields and farm-lands, high hedges and stretches of woodlands with familiar English trees. On the coast are fishing villages, watering-places and old towns such as Sönderborg and Fredericia. The most important town is Aarhus, capital of Jutland and the next largest city after Copenhagen. Aarhus is a cathedral and university city as well as a commercial port. It has in the 'Old Town' an open-air museum where old houses, old furniture, workshops and handicrafts recall life in Denmark during the past three hundred years. Among the city's modern attractions is a large stadium. To the south of the city, in a woodland setting, is the Royal Palace of Marselisborg, the summer residence of the King and Queen who received it as a wedding present from the Danish people. Away to the west, in central Jutland, are a series of lakes famous for the abundance of water lilies which grow in them. Towards the western end of this lakeland, near Silkeborg, is Himmelbjerg, 'The Heavenly Moun-tain', a hill of 550 feet and the second largest in Denmark. It is of historic interest as an ancient place of popular assembly.

Viborg, in the heart of Jutland, standing above a blue-green lake, is an ancient town near the ruins of one of the oldest of Danish castles, the castle of Hald.

The extreme north of Jutland is separated from the rest of the peninsula by the Lim Fjord on which is situated the great port of Aalborg, and which penetrates the coast as a wide and tortuous water-way, flowing right across to the east coast.

North of the fjord the peninsula gradually

narrows to the spit of land known as the Skaw where the tides of the Skagerrak and the Kattegat meet. Here are lines of curiously shaped sand dunes interspersed with dry grass, and farther to the south is the greatest unchecked sand drift in Jutland. Built on both sides of the Skaw is Skagen, one of the largest fishing towns in Denmark and inhabited by a hardy people who have beeh compared to the old Vikings. The town, however, has lately become fashionable as a holiday centre and hotels have been built to accommodate the summer visitors who come here for the good bathing and sandy beaches.

FÜNEN. The island of Fünen, which lies between Jutland and Zealand, has a countryside very like some of the well-wooded parts of southern England. Lanes such as one finds in Hampshire or Surrey lead to pleasant villages where some of the houses date from the eighteenth century or earlier. The farms seen across the fields often take on the appearance of small hamlets. The coast is mostly sheltered and the narrow seas between Fünen and Jutland, and between Fünen and the island of Langeland in the south-east, look like wide rivers, especially where the woods come down almost to the shore. The extreme north, however, is wilder, especially on the long peninsula of Hindsholm, the home of many kinds of sea birds.

There are many small towns and villages round the coast of Fünen, but the capital of the island, Odense, lies inland with a harbour on Odense Fjord. This ancient town takes its name from the god Odin and had considerable importance in early

Danish history. To many visitors, however, it is chiefly interesting as the birthplace of Hans Andersen. Hans Andersen's father, an impoverished and sickly shoemaker, made his home in one room of a cottage, and this small house is now preserved as a national museum. Some of the furniture from the writer's lodgings in Copenhagen has been brought here, and some of his personal belongings are also preserved for the pleasure of visitors.

ZEALAND. Zealand is the largest and most important of the Danish islands. Its level landscape, occasionally broken with little hills, presents constant views of woodland and water, especially in the north where fjords penetrate deep into the island and where there are also a number of small lakes. It is linked up with the rest of the country by the ships which come and go from its various ports, and a railway system criss-crosses the island, connecting the main towns with each other and with Copenhagen. One of the regular routes from Great Britain to the Danish capital runs directly across from west to east. By this route the traveller disembarks at Esbjerg and travels by rail right across both Jutland and Fünen (joined by the long railway bridge) and then by train ferry across the Great Belt to Korsör, whence the last stage of the railway journey brings him to Copenhagen.

An alternative is to take an all-sea route round the north of Jutland, through the wide seaway of the Kattegat, and then through the Sound which separates Sweden and Denmark.

In the last hour or so of this journey, the very close proximity of Sweden and Denmark is brought home to any stranger, for as the ship travels through the narrow channel between Elsinore and Halsingborg the two countries appear to be on opposite sides of a wide river, and even after the Sound widens towards the Baltic, the Swedish coast is still visible. The Danish coast is wooded and scattered with villas, and on the way from Elsinore to Copenhagen all kinds of commercial and pleasure craft are met, including racing yachts when the weather is suitable.

COPENHAGEN. Copenhagen, the one really large city of Denmark (it holds a fourth of the whole population of the country), is a city of waterways. Partly built on the Zealand coast and partly on a neighbouring island, it is intersected by arms of the sea as well as by canals. It is a port and ship-building centre of the first importance with the largest ice-free harbour in northern Europe. It is also a University city and Denmark's most vital industrial area. Although of ancient origin it has been partly destroyed by fire so often that few very old buildings remain. It has, nevertheless, in its older quarter the narrow and winding streets of earlier times, while the wide thoroughfares and modern buildings make the new town in some respects characteristic of western Europe. Copenhagen comprises three municipalities, that of Copenhagen proper and those of Frederiksberg and Gentofte. Like Oxford it is known as the City of Spires, and it is a place of peculiar charm, due rather to the happy combination of masonry, sky and water than to particular architectural merits. The Old Exchange, and other buildings in 'the style of Christian IV', possess, however, an intimate beauty of their own. A number of museums and art collections have an international reputation. The great Danish breweries have established important foundations for the promotion of the arts. The visitor is always surprised at the great number of cycles to be seen on the streets, for everyone rides a bicycle—including members of the Royal Family. The most popular pleasure resort is the amusement park, known as the Tivoli Gardens, open from May until mid-September in each year. The gardens were laid out in 1843 on part of the former ramparts and contain a concert hall, a theatre, a stage for acrobatic performances, a dance hall, sideshows, and a number of cafés and restaurants all set among trees and brilliant flower beds. There is also a lake, which was once part of the town moat.

BORNHOLM. The island of Bornholm, which is roughly the size of the Isle of Man, is an eight hours' sea passage across the Baltic from Copenhagen. It has a coast of curious granite formations with caves into which small boats can penetrate in calm weather. The interior is mostly a plateau, rising to its highest point in the centre of the island where there is a large forest which is State property. The people are mainly occupied with agriculture or fishing, or labour in the granite works, and live either in isolated farmsteads or in one of the market towns. A feature of the island is the variety of its vegetation; many of the flowers which grow here are not commonly seen except in the mountains of central or southern Europe.

THE FAEROE ISLANDS. 'These islands of Faeroe', wrote a seventeenth-century commentator, 'lying in the midst of the storming sea, far distant from other countryes, have, during a long time, been uninhabited, being only visited by the fowles of Heaven.' The description is appropriate, for the islands rise with steep and menacing cliffs from the North Atlantic, and thousands of sea birds haunt the coasts. They are situated between Iceland and the Shetlands, but at considerable distance from both. There are twenty-one islands in the group—excluding those which are barren rocks—but only seventeen are inhabited. Despite the semi-arctic latitude, the climate is warmer than in some parts of Scotland, but the winter, although not excessively cold, is a time of hurricanes and thunderstorms which brings most out-door occupations to a standstill.

The islands are treeless, except for plantations of conifers introduced by the Danes, and the rugged nature of the ground makes it mostly unfit for ploughing, so that agriculture is pursued by humble methods, as well as on a very limited scale. There are little patches of earth on which barley is cultivated, and there is considerable grassland and pasture for sheep. Sheep-rearing, the production of root crops, whaling and cod fishing and industries connected with them are the chief occupations of the inhabitants. There is also good shooting of the eider duck and other wild fowls.

GREENLAND. The immense island of Greenland, fifty times the size of Denmark, lies close to the Canadian island of Ellesmere in the Arctic Ocean.

All the interior of the country is permanently frozen under an ice cap or glacier, so deep that all but a few of the interior mountain peaks are buried beneath it. The only inhabited part lies on, or near, the mountainous and indented south and west coasts—about one-twentieth of the whole. Here are Esquimaux settlements consisting of stone and turf huts, each entered by a long tunnel. The few Danish traders and administrators import wood for their homes and cover it with pitch. The trade of the colony is a State monopoly and the exports consist chiefly of fish oil, skins, eiderdown and cryolite.

ICELAND

As Iceland was Danish territory until June 17, 1944, when, following a decision of the island's national assembly, the last link with Denmark was broken (it was already self-governing) it is appropriate to conclude this chapter with some mention of the country.

The island lies in the North Atlantic, off the east coast of Greenland, and is about two-and-a-half times the size of Denmark. It is of exceptional geographical and historical interest; the Icelandic Sagas, which tell of the early settlements of the Norsemen, are one of the richest treasures of the primitive literature of northern Europeans. The striking physical feature of the island is its combination of volcanic heat and glacial cold. There are over one hundred volcanoes and twenty-five have erupted within human memory; the most recent serious outbreak occurred in 1934. The volcanoes rise in the great icefields which cover most of the high interior of the country, and an eruption will sometimes send a glacier sliding down towards the coast. The best known icefield is Vatna Jökull, in the south-east. Its name means 'the glacier which gives water', for torrential rivers pour out from underneath its ice walls, melted by the volcanic heat below, and carrying rocks and stones in their courses.

North of Vatna Jökull there is a barren waste, reaching to the north coast and strewn with twisted lava, gravel, pumice stone and dust. The same kind of forbidding landscape is found in the centre and south-west of the island. Here and there are lakes which have formed in extinct craters and in hollows in the valleys.

The 130,000 inhabitants live on the coast or on the grassy plains a little inland, but one-third of them are found in Reykjavik, the capital, on the south-west coast. The most fertile plain stretches from Reykjavik for sixty miles as far as Geysir, where there are hot springs, one of which sometimes sends up a spout of water 70 metres high. Other warm springs are found in other parts of the island. The life of the people, who are remarkable for their civilization and education, is a constant struggle against the weather. Sheep-rearing and fishing are the chief occupations; the annual catch of fish (cod and herring) works out at 4914 pounds per head. There are no railways in the country and some of the coastal townships are only accessible by sea, but a few good roads have been built, and the different parts of the island are linked by telephone and telegraph. Even remote farms usually have electric light, derived from local water power, and wireless sets, which receive transmissions from a station in the capital.

CHAPTER III

LIFE AND WORK OF THE
DANISH PEOPLE

THE STANDARD OF LIVING. Visitors to Denmark are usually impressed by the absence of poverty in the country, and the Danes themselves often claim that they have realized the economic idea of democracy described by Grundtvig: 'Few people have too much and fewer too little.' Along with this high standard of living there is a high standard of education. Compulsory schooling was introduced as long ago as 1814 and Denmark has long been a pioneer in adult education. Most Danish people therefore live—in normal times—in relative comfort and are well-informed. There are no illiterates. The country has more radio sets and more telephones in proportion to the population than any other country in Europe. Foreigners are made welcome, and there is hardly a village throughout Denmark in which an Englishman could not exchange some conversation in his own language.

A third of the Danish people live on the land, but technical developments in agriculture have caused the old peasant life, with its simple implements and handicrafts, to disappear into the museums. Except in a few fishing villages, and on the island of Amager, near Copenhagen, the old peasant furniture and interior decoration are seldom seen, and the wearing of the traditional

peasant dress was discontinued in nearly every part
of the country some fifty years ago. Modern manu-
facturers, however, have begun to draw inspiration
from ancient Danish craftsmanship, and a movement is on foot to restore the designs of the old
handwoven cloth and embroideries and to adapt
them to modern requirements.

FARM LIFE. A great many old buildings, however,
remain, including farmhouses built of clay walls
and timber. Half-timbered walls are characteristic
of farmhouses in some parts of the country. Most
of these old farms consist of four thatched buildings,
standing in a square, enclosing a courtyard, with
the dwelling-house facing south. Whether living
in one of these old houses or in a modern home
of red brick and tiles the Danish farmer works
hard. Generally speaking, work on a farm starts,
as in this country, at five in the morning with the
milking of the cows and grooming of horses,
followed by the feeding of the animals. Then comes
a first breakfast, consisting only of a cup of coffee
or tea and some bread and marmalade or jam. At
8.30 or 9 a.m., after the cleaning of the stables and
byres and other early morning jobs, there is a more
substantial breakfast with hot porridge or a fish dish
(this varies according to the part of the country
in which he lives); sandwiches are provided for
those who are working too far from the farm to
get home for this. The break lasts for only half
an hour, after which work is carried on until
the midday interval for lunch, which lasts from
one to one and a half hours. This is the main meal
of the day, and it usually consists of two courses

and coffee. Most farmers and their assistants then have half an hour's sleep before they resume work, since they have all risen at an early hour. If it can be fitted in with the jobs in hand, there is usually a cup of coffee to be had in the afternoon between 3 and 4 o'clock. Work stops at 5, 6 or 7 p.m. according to the season; during the harvests it may even continue in the night with the help of artificial light.

Owing to the co-operative system there is not so much individual marketing done in Denmark as there is in England, although horse-dealing is an exception and is usually done privately by individual farmers rather than by the co-operatives. For those farmers who go in for horse-dealing the market days are the high spots of the year.

Just after the New Year, a festive season in Denmark, the annual meetings of the Co-operative Societies take place, and are spread over the first three months of the year at a time when farm work is at its slackest. The farmers then go to town to hear the results of the year's work and also to hear about the latest developments in agricultural science and economics. On these occasions the wives accompany their husbands, taking the opportunity to do shopping and to visit places of entertainment in the evening.

HOLIDAYS. Denmark enjoys a number of national holidays. Danish Constitution Day, on June 5, and Danish Flag Day, June 15, are celebrated by patriotic and political meetings throughout the country. At this time of year Parliament is not in session and politicians take the opportunity of meeting their constituents. The meetings usually end with an open-air dance, or some other form of entertainment. On June 23 midsummer day is celebrated in town and country alike by the lighting of bonfires and many forms of entertainment. Another welcome break comes in the autumn with the celebration on September 26 of the King's birthday. On this day, as on Constitution Day and Flag Day, the children have a school holiday, and in Copenhagen they are prominently to the fore. From early in the morning they may be seen gathering together in the great square before the Royal Palace, where they cheer the King, who usually obliges the young citizens of Denmark by appearing from time to time on the balcony. November 10 is St Martin's Day, which is always observed as a family festival: on this day there is usually goose for dinner. The great festival of the year is, of course, Christmas. The main celebrations take place on Christmas Eve, when after the traditional dinner of rice, roast goose and apple tart, usually served at about 6 p.m., the Christmas tree is lighted and presents distributed. In February the carnival season begins and lasts until the first Monday in Lent. That day is a public holiday in rural Denmark, with gymkhanas at which young men display their horsemanship. The girls watch, and those who do best in the ring are usually also those who are best off for partners at the balls which are held in the evening. The children dress up and go round singing for pennies, and they are generally asked for repeat performances. At Easter time there are four holidays with church services.

SPORTS. Denmark's national sport to-day is undoubtedly football—association football, for rugby
is unknown there. Physical culture is enthusias-
tically pursued throughout the country; practically
all villages and towns have clubs for this purpose.
The most famous method is the Niels Bukh
system of 'primitive gymnastics', which has sup-
planted to a very large extent the older and more
formal gymnastics systems. Swimming, both in-
door and open air, has developed enormously in
recent years. Open-air swimming pools were being
built on an impressive scale throughout the country
before the war, although it is true that most of
the population has more or less easy access to sea
bathing. Cricket is played on a small scale. Bad-
minton and handball are popular with both sexes.
A good deal of tennis is played, but this is an
expensive entertainment in which not everyone can
indulge. There are also a few golf courses. A fair
number of young people engage in light athletics,
but it must be admitted that many more prefer to
be spectators. Sailing and boating are very popular,
since Denmark provides every facility for these
recreations. Horse racing is becoming more and
more popular.

EDUCATION. By law a Dane must receive education from the 7th to the 14th year. Some 90 %
of the elementary schools are run by the municipal
authorities; the rest are private enterprises. At the
age of 11 a child is eligible to receive the first stages
of senior education by attending one of the inter-
mediate schools, at which he continues until the
age of 15. Then, provided the necessary examina-

tion is passed, he can proceed to the Grammar School or other senior school where he stays until he is 18. At the end of this period the successful passing of matriculation admits him to the university.

Those young people who elect to enter one of the Government services or who choose a commercial career usually leave school at the age of 15, but, at this stage, in connexion with a practical training or apprenticeship, they are given an intensive theoretical education to fit them for their work in life. A successful apprenticeship enables a young person to continue his education at a commercial college.

Senior education is to a large extent supplied by the municipal authorities, but some institutions are owned by the State. Universities are wholly State institutions. The whole educational system enables the young Danish citizen to receive his education at every stage practically free of charge.

THE FOLK HIGH SCHOOLS. General and technical education are both on an exceptionally high level—even a workman cannot receive recognition as being skilled at his job until the necessary examinations have been passed—and are designed to fit those educated for practical life. Adult education, however, is exemplified in the Folk High Schools, which have no utilitarian purpose in view. They exist to stimulate and enlighten, they try to educate for life and not for gaining a living. They provide no 'academic labels', for they award no diplomas and hold no examinations.

These schools were conceived by the famous Danish patriot, N. F. S. Grundtvig, 'the prophet of the North', as he was called by the Germans of his day. His ideas of liberal folk education were expressed simply: 'To make accessible to young people a place where they may become better acquainted with human nature and human life in general, and with themselves in particular, and where they will receive guidance in all civic duties and relationships and get to know the real needs of their country.' The first Folk High School was opened 100 years ago.

At first these schools were viewed by many with little favour. Some people laughed at them; others frowned. The privileged classes did not relish giving the ordinary people 'too much education'. The notorious *Stavnsbaand*, which bound the peasant to the county in which he was born, and the object of which had been to provide land-owners with farm hands and tenant farmers as well as with the soldiers they were obliged to provide the Crown, had been dissolved. The peasant was now a free man, and it was feared that the rural population, after receiving an education, would become too good to plough, dig ditches, and spread manure. In the event, the free peasant put these ideas to shame: his schools did not teach him to despise the land, but instead inspired him to make a really sound job of his farming. For Grundtvig and his pioneers of the Folk High Schools were united in seeing nothing particularly elegant in being wealthy, and they saw nothing base in poverty unless this was accompanied by ignorance and immorality.

The Folk High Schools are in theory and practice entirely different from any other school for adult education. They are residential and the students go to them of their own free will. A few run co-educational courses, but most have a five months' winter course for young men and a three months' summer course for young women. As already mentioned they are in no sense vocational. Students are not qualified for certain positions because they have attended a Folk High School. Practically all the students go back to their own work, but they generally do so with a changed outlook on life and a knowledge of the part they are expected to play in the development of a working community.

The schools are designed not to choke the mind with 'dead letters', but to open the door of the mind and set the spirit free. Curriculum, teaching, spiritual and social life at the school, all hang together.

The schools aim to give the young men and women attending them a historical-political background for their lives. Instruction is given in the Danish language, for a proper understanding of the Danish tongue is held to be vital to all. The history of mankind, the development of spiritual values, poetry and art are the subjects of lectures at these schools. Instruction is oral, the teacher endeavouring to inspire his hearers by means of what Grundtvig called 'the living word'.

There are now sixty Folk High Schools in Denmark, and some 7000 pupils pass through them each year. The sexes are almost evenly divided, and their ages range between 16 and 25. Most of them come from the rural areas and are the sons and daughters of farmers. Tuition, board and lodging cost the student about £4. 0s. 0d. per month.

Although practically all Folk High Schools are located in rural Denmark, a few are found in the cities. There is one such school in Copenhagen (Borup's Folk High School) with lectures open also to the general public, but it differs from most because it is not a residential school. There are two other similar schools for workers, one in Roskilde and one in Esbjerg, attended mostly by workers in and around these towns.

During the past thirty years one-third of Danish agricultural youth has passed through the Folk High Schools, or through the Agricultural High Schools (run on similar lines), of which the first was opened in 1840. Of these there were twenty-one in 1938, with about 2600 students.

It should also be mentioned that Peter Manniche, before the war, ran an International Folk High School at Elsinore, near Copenhagen, with an international teaching staff and pupils from all over the world. This school stresses particularly the need for international understanding. It is founded upon and inspired by the ideals of the Folk High Schools, being, like these, individualistic in educational principles, ethical in purpose, and seeking to apply the rules of Christianity in individual and social life.

SOCIAL SERVICES. Denmark was not untouched by the industrial revolution (although approximately one-third of the population still lives by agriculture) and therefore, in the latter part of the nineteenth century, trade unions made their appearance there. The organized workers demanded improved living conditions for city workers, and numerous social reforms eventually brought these into existence. There is an extensive system of social security, with unemployment and accident insurances, old age pensions and free medical services.

By using all technical improvements of modern times living conditions are now everywhere on a very high standard. The meanest cottage in the country has electric light, and modern sanitation is in general use. The ordinary man is possessed of reasonable comforts.

ART. It may be partly due to the high standard of living that the ordinary citizen in Denmark takes a great interest in art and in the preservation of the country's historic treasures. Danish museums and art galleries are visited by thousands of people every year. It is not without significance that it is to a man of the people, the brewer J. C. Jacobsen, that the Danish nation is indebted for the preservation of many of its treasures, and that these are well displayed and always on view to the public. It is, for instance, chiefly due to the initiative of Jacobsen that the Museum of National History at Frederiksborg, the old hunting castle of King Frederick II, still retains its character. The collections there on view are arranged in such a way that they show Danish history through the ages, with portraits of each King and his period, and with furniture and art treasures in contemporary style.

Amongst the many Danish museums the unique open-air museum at Lyngby, outside Copenhagen, deserves special mention. Here there are groups of ancient rural buildings, some dating back to the Middle Ages, transported to the spot from many distant parts of the country. Similar to this is the 'Old Town' at Aarhus, which has already been mentioned.

The most important collection of Danish paintings and etchings is to be found, with foreign collections, at the State Museum of Art, though it must be admitted that Denmark has never produced an artist of world fame, with the possible exception of the sculptor Thorvaldsen. Neither have the Danes produced a great musician. Danish music generally is mild, friendly, and reminiscent of folk song. To a Dane song is as essential as string music to a gipsy.

The Danes are great readers. Libraries abound in the country. The best known of these is perhaps the Copenhagen University Library, founded in 1482, and extraordinarily rich in ancient Danish and foreign manuscripts and in Norse and Icelandic literature.

RECREATION. The Danish city workers in industry and commerce do not, generally speaking, enjoy the English week-end: except in rare cases they have to work as usual on Saturdays and have only their Sundays free. Government offices are also open on Saturday afternoons. The eight-hour day, however, is almost universally in force. The people often spend their leisure hours walking and cycling. Hiking was before the war so popular that many of the national newspapers made a point of sketching out walks for their readers to take on Sundays.

To almost every Dane his bicycle is his best friend, which will take him everywhere and which he can transport almost everywhere. In Denmark people cycle to work and back. And the same people go off on their cycles on Sunday mornings along the roads leading out of town—particularly in summer those leading to the nearest bathing beaches. People living in cities often carry their camp equipment with them, when they set out late on Saturday, intending to stay the night in some secluded place known to them, or else to go to one of the great camping grounds, usually along the seaboard, most of which are little communities with rules of their own.

In the larger cities such as Copenhagen the greater part of the population lives in flats. But on the outskirts of the towns are groups of allotments where most people erect a little wooden bungalow in which it is possible for the family to live in summer time, or where they can at any rate spend their week-ends. In these gardens are grown vegetables, fruit, and flowers to supply the household, and they are a source of great pleasure to their owners. The cost of a plot is very small, being really within the reach of anyone who wants one. They vary in size, so that the less energetic can take smaller plots and still have their home-grown produce.

The Danes are essentially a peace-loving people, hard-working and without envy of their greater neighbours. They have no desire for national expansion, but concern themselves rather with the arts of living gracefully and improving their standards at home. A British Member of Parliament aptly summed them up when he wrote[1]:

'To most English people Denmark and the Danes mean a place and a people who produce eggs, bacon and butter with great efficiency and devastating cheapness.... Denmark (in fact) means some of the most up-to-date ship-building and diesel-engine plants in the world, it means lovely old castles, it means a vast variety of extraordinarily good food, it means the home of the best cherry brandy in the world, it means the charm of Copenhagen, with wonderful book-shops, better than those of London and New York, it means a nation more highly educated in the mass than any other national group, it means efficiency without dullness, it means a social state which has achieved true democratic standards.'

[1] Commander Stephen King-Hall in *Free Denmark*, August, 1942.

CHAPTER IV

THE ECONOMY OF DENMARK

DEVELOPMENT OF DANISH ECONOMY. Because of
Danish bacon and butter many people believe that
Denmark is mainly an agricultural country. The
fact is, however, that only approximately one-
third of the people live by agriculture. From time
immemorial shipping has been of primary importance in Denmark, and Danish industry has
reached a high state of development, and, with
handicrafts, gives employment to just over one-
third of the population.

In the latter half of the eighteenth century
Denmark enjoyed a golden age of trade. It was a
time when most of the European countries were
involved in wars, and Denmark's neutral attitude
and her fleet of merchant vessels made Copenhagen
a centre of trade in the Baltic. Great companies
were formed and considerable fortunes were made
right up to 1807, when Denmark also became involved in war and the golden era came to an
abrupt end. The crisis was the more severely felt
because Denmark's trade was founded on foreign
markets and there was no home market to absorb
a sudden flow of goods. Agriculture was not yet
developed and industry was in its infancy. The
population numbered barely a million souls all
told. All these factors help to explain the collapse
of Danish commerce in the first part of the

nineteenth century. Hamburg consequently ousted Copenhagen from her position as queen of the north European ports. The Hanseatic cities of Hamburg and Lübeck reaped the benefit of Copenhagen's weakness even in regard to Denmark's own import trade, and matters continued thus until the war between Denmark and Germany in 1848–50.

In the fifties Denmark's commercial life took a turn for the better. Danish farmers began to feel the beneficial results of agricultural legislation which had already been passed two generations before. England adopted free trade. The Danish national spirit was aroused by the war with Germany. Danish trade emancipated itself from its dependence on Hamburg and took an increasing interest in England, both as regards exports and imports. In 1848 a direct steamer service was opened between Jutland and England.

In the years 1850–75 Denmark was still a corn-growing country, with cattle and butter gradually becoming more and more important. This was still the period when butter was tasted before it was bought from the farmer and exchanged by the market-town merchant for groceries. Merchants' premises had to serve as a sort of guest-house, shop, and bank for the farmers. In the seventies American wheat competition put a stop to Denmark's agricultural export trade. Denmark, moreover, had been defeated by Prussia in 1864 and had lost the province of Schleswig Holstein. Just at the time when the United States began to flood Europe with their huge abundance of corn, Germany made her first effort to establish herself as an empire. This development was one reason why protectionism made its entry into many European countries, and why industrial production increased enormously. England, Holland and Denmark, however, remained as upholders of free trade, and instead of protecting agriculture by tariffs the Danish farmers gave up growing wheat and concentrated on the production of butter, bacon and eggs for the English market. These developments, already mentioned in Chapter I, ran parallel with a national and political awakening in Denmark, and an educational foundation was laid which made possible the introduction of co-operation and scientific methods in farming.

After the loss of Schleswig Holstein the Danes started a great work of land reclamation, which made room for many new farms. Barren heath or moor were turned into cultivated land. Defeat on the field of battle was, in fact, followed by remarkable achievements.

This development of Danish agriculture was continued until the outbreak of the second world war, when Denmark's agricultural resources were exploited by the Germans after they occupied the country on April 9, 1940.

THE CO-OPERATIVE SYSTEM. Denmark became a supplier to the world of more butter and eggs than any other country. Of the international trade in bacon and hams, Denmark's share was one-half and in butter and eggs it was one-quarter. Immediately before the war 83 % of Denmark's butter production and 64 % of her bacon production were sold abroad. Co-operation had led Denmark to the highest degree of agricultural efficiency. The co-operative system is a voluntary one. It developed amongst the farmers themselves, proceeding hand in hand with their educational enlightenment. The secret of the success of this system is that it enabled the small farmer to place his output as advantageously as the large-scale farmer. This is exemplified, for instance, in the case of the co-operative dairy. The milk collector calls at every farm, large or small, and at the dairy all the milk is poured into one container. It undoubtedly needed foresight and a measure of self-sacrifice to make the change-over to co-operation. In 1882 the first Danish co-operative dairy was established for the purpose of handling milk for a group of farmers on a co-operative basis. It was at this time that the milk separator made its appearance. To-day about 92 % of all Danish farmers are members of a co-operative dairy. This system gives the butter an even quality which is of the greatest importance for its marketing. Some 85 % of all Danish bacon is produced in co-operative enterprises, and excellent fat cattle for export are also to a great extent handled by co-operatives. The causes favouring the co-operative system in Denmark are varied. The great number of livestock concentrated in a small area makes it possible to subject the produce, and particularly milk, to a uniform treatment. A well-developed system of roads facilitates the transport of milk to the dairies; and the extensive network of railways enables easy transport of pigs to the bacon factories to be made. Thanks to the educational enlightenment of the farmers they are able to find amongst themselves their own representatives to whom they can entrust the interest of local co-operative concerns. It is worth mentioning that voting rights at all meetings of the societies allow one vote only to each member, regardless of the amount of goods supplied by him.

The co-operative fellowships are created in order to secure to the individual producer the best prices for his products, regardless of quantity, but based on quality. The individual co-operative undertakings are combined in central organizations which, by means of scientific methods, see to it that the total production of the country is placed on the highest possible level of quality. They are also concerned with placing the produce on foreign markets. Out of the Folk High Schools Agricultural Colleges have developed, and there are now many technical journals dealing exclusively with farming affairs, even the smallest smallholder being a regular reader of at least one of these publications. There are 139 farmers' associations and 1323 smallholders' associations, and these arrange agricultural shows, make tests, and employ agricultural advisers. The Royal Danish Agricultural Society is the oldest existing association, having been established in 1769. The Agricultural Council was inaugurated in 1919 and is the central organization for practically all organized agriculture, representing agricultural interests in negotiations with the Government and with outside trades and industries.

Many breeding and milk control societies have been formed. Every cow of every member of a control society is regularly examined in regard to its feeding, milk yield, and amount of butter fat per gallon. Moreover, the Government guarantees that all butter exported from Denmark is made of pasteurized cream and contains 80 % butter fat, not more than 16 % water and no preservative other than common salt.

Denmark has 1730 dairies, of which no fewer than 1400 are co-operative. A few figures may serve to show the remarkable strides made by Danish dairy farmers in the course of less than a century. In 1864 the yield of butter per cow was 80 lb.; in 1887 it was 116 lb.; in 1908 it was 220 lb.; and in 1929 it had reached 317 lb. In 1943 the figure for the record cow was 1140 lb. This cow gave 15,800 lb. of milk with a 6·2 % butter-fat content.

The production of bacon is closely allied to the dairy industry. Skimmed milk and butter milk is returned from the dairy to the farms, where it is fed to the pigs. This feeding produces the kind of bacon required by the English market. When the pigs are six months old and weigh just under 200 lb. they are ready for the bacon factories, of which sixty-two are co-operative as compared with twenty-two private concerns.

Before the war grain was grown principally as feed for livestock, much of the grain-growing area being sown with mixed crops (mostly barley and oats grown together) which are unfit for human consumption. Potatoes and other root crops occupy a considerable area. Fodder beets and home-grown green fodder are extensively used for cattle feed, and are supplemented with imported oil cakes. The bread grain consumed in the country was largely imported.

INDUSTRIES. Denmark possesses no raw materials such as coal, oil, iron, or other minerals. Neither has she the valuable pine and fir forests of Norway, Sweden and Finland, nor great rivers and waterfalls to turn into sources of power. Yet just over a third of her population lives by industry and skilled handicrafts. As stated in a previous chapter, old handicraft traditions have been preserved in modern production, and have imparted to this an essence of quality and personal taste. The industries all grew up around the towns: in Denmark there are no industrial towns as such. Few countries have such an extensive coastline, and consequently such easy access to the sea—and safe and good harbours mean also easy and cheap conveyance of raw materials into the country and manufactures out of it. The ports have therefore become the natural seats of the greater part of the industrial plants. In only a few cases has native raw material played an important part, and with regard to some of these—notably the great cement works—the fortunate circumstance was that the raw materials were at hand near the coast. Thus the two large centres of cement production are placed around Aalborg and Mariager in Jutland, where one large factory stands alongside another close to the sea, and with their own harbours and loading places. The sole remaining requirement was their manufacturing and marketing on a profitable basis.

EXPORTS. The foremost task of Danish industry is to supply the home market, but, in course of time, no small number of articles made in Denmark have secured a market beyond the country's frontiers. The guiding principle has been to turn out goods of high quality so as to establish a good name for Danish products outside Denmark, and thus, hand in hand with the home industries, to build up a considerable export trade. Denmark specializes in high-quality goods rather than in mass production.

The value of industrial exports rose from 196 million Kroner in 1933 to 252 million Kroner in 1934. Industrial production between 1928 and 1939 increased by 50 %. In the years 1931–2 there was a considerable decrease in industrial production. Industrial exports in the years 1928–30 averaged 300 million Kroner a year, but in 1932 declined to 200 million Kroner. They rose in 1937 to 400 million Kroner.

In the sphere of engineering the firms of Burmeister and Wain and F. L. Smidth and Co. held almost a world monopoly as makers of special machinery. In 1912 Burmeister and Wain built the world's first ocean-going motor ship, the *Selandia*, for the Danish East Asiatic Company, and since then Burmeister and Wain motors have become the foremost throughout international shipbuilding. In 1939 42 % of the motor ships on the high seas used Danish diesel engines. Frichs, Ltd., in Aarhus, have started the making of electric locomotives. In the building and running of cement works F. L. Smidth and Co. have led the way. The enormous demand for cement has not only resulted in the export of Danish-made cement, but also in the growth of a Danish cement machine industry which has become the largest and best known in the world.

The oil industry is also of considerable importance in Denmark's export trade, and in some years has even represented one-third of all the country's industrial exports. Among the principal products of this industry are vegetable oils and solidified fats made from these, for which two large mills, the Aarhus Oliefabrik, Ltd. and the Dansk Sojakagefabrik, receive their raw materials from plantations in the tropics. It is mainly the margarine works which use these oils, and agriculture absorbs the rest of the output for cattle cake and other fodder. Mutual exchange of experience between producers in agriculture and industry has resulted in a high standard of quality not only in foodstuffs, but also in the machines and apparatus used in their production. Thus Danish dairy machines and slaughterhouse equipment follow in the train of Danish butter and bacon. Condensed milk is a commodity which has become one of Denmark's great export articles, and it is scarcely possible to see anywhere else in the world to-day the automatic handling of food carried through so consistently as in this branch, where every process is automatic, without the milk being touched by human hands. The same is the case with Danish tinned hams.

The production of medicines is another industry with roots in Danish agriculture. Besides many of purely synthetic origin, Denmark now makes a number of pure, carefully standardized organotherapeutic preparations which have been widely adopted by medical science in recent years. This industry receives a high proportion of its raw materials from Danish model slaughter houses.

The list of export articles includes also every-day consumption goods such as Danish vacuum cleaners, manufactured by Fisker and Nielsen. Still greater success has been recorded by Danish dry-cell batteries, which, under the name of Hellesen, are known throughout the world. This concern has more than 100,000 distributors, spread over all five continents.

The art industry has developed considerably, and principally includes the famous silverware and porcelain bearing the mark of many generations. The silversmiths, Georg Jensen Co., and the two great porcelain works in Copenhagen, the Royal Porcelain Co. and Bing and Groendahl, have succeeded in building up a connexion of international connoisseurs as customers.

As a whole, the relatively high purchasing power of the Danish population and its profound realization that the best is always the cheapest, has found its reflexion in Danish industry, which bases all its products upon the criterion of quality.

A remarkable feature of Danish technical activity is the role played by Danish civil and constructing engineers. In practically all branches of engineering construction, and particularly in bridge building, harbour works, railways, industrial and other building construction, Danish engineers have made themselves prominent. Much of the credit for this success must be given to the high standard of the State College of Engineering in Copenhagen. The standard of the industrial workers is also high. During the period of their apprenticeship they must study at industrial night schools for a number of years, and they receive no recognition as skilled workers until they have passed their practical as well as theoretical examinations.

SHIPPING. Along with the Norwegian, the Danish merchant fleet holds the lead in the general transition from steam to motor power. Leaders of Danish shipping play a vital part in the economic life of the country. Although Danish officers and men are paid good wages and State subsidies are unknown, Danish shipping has been able to compete successfully in the international market. In 1937, for instance, Danish ships carried some 9,000,000 tons of freight between foreign countries, without touching home ports. Of the total profits of the Danish mercantile marine some two-thirds are earned in foreign trade.

The Danes have been a sea-going people ever since the days of the Vikings. The nature of the country made ships a natural means of conveyance.

FISHERIES. During the past forty years the fisheries have become a valuable source of income, and in 1938 fishermen were using no fewer than 6480 motor vessels. Many of these fishermen brought their catches to the shores of Britain before the war, and convoys of lorries conveyed other catches to Germany and France. Danish trout were formerly served in French restaurants.

During the war over 400 fishermen escaped to England with about 70 trawlers. Some of their ships have continued to help in provisioning Britain, and others have been taken over by the Admiralty and used as balloon ships.

Chapter V

DENMARK UNDER THE GERMANS (1)

On May 31, 1939, five months before the war
started, Denmark reluctantly accepted an invita-
tion from Hitler to sign a non-aggression pact.
The first paragraph of this pact reads:

'The Kingdom of Denmark and the German
Reich will in no circumstances go to war and
neither will they in any other way resort to force
against each other.'

On April 9, 1940, when the pact was only ten
months old, Hitler ordered his armies to occupy
Denmark.

Denmark had already realized that this time it
would be even more difficult than it was in the last
world war to go on trading with both belligerents
and to maintain neutrality. On the eve of the
outbreak of war Hitler sent a special emissary,
Minister von Hassel, to Copenhagen to renew the
promise already given that Denmark could continue her usual trade with Britain and other countries hostile to Germany, provided she continued
also to trade with the Germans. A few months
later, however, Hitler announced that 'to sail to
England was to sail to death'. In spite of the constant danger from German U-boats and bombers,
Denmark went on supplying Britain, her old cus-
tomer, with the food she needed. By April 9,
when the Germans put a final stop to all connexions

westwards, about forty great ships had been sunk in the North Sea.

THE GERMAN INVASION. When the Germans presented their ultimatum to the Danish Government there were only 25,000 men under arms in Denmark. Serious warnings had been sent at the beginning of April to the Danish Government in Copenhagen by the Danish Minister in Berlin, Mr Zahle, who declared that an invasion was imminent, and there had also been a flow of reports from Schleswig-Holstein to the effect that great troop concentrations were being assembled. But when the Danish Commander-in-Chief, General Prior, asked for general mobilization the Government refused because the German Minister, Herr von Renthe Fink, had clearly told the Foreign Minister, Dr Munch, that any such step would be taken as an act of hostility towards Germany. A State Council meeting was held in the early morning of April 9, at Amalienborg Castle, to discuss the German ultimatum. The Prime Minister, the Minister of Foreign Affairs, the Minister of Defence, and the two chiefs of the services were present, and the King presided. As they deliberated a great formation of German bombers droned over the capital and the German Minister made it plain that orders to obliterate Copenhagen would be given if the ultimatum was not accepted. Before the Ministers were reliable reports that British political leaders had recently expressed the view that Britain could not come to the assistance of Denmark if she were attacked, and resistance by the Danish army was held to be hopeless. Den-

mark would thus find herself in a similar position
to that which faced her in 1864, when she alone
was the first victim of German imperialism. The
Danish Government, in the period between the
two wars, had followed a policy of disarmament.
The King, therefore, supported by his ministers,
but against the advice of General Prior, decided
to submit to the German ultimatum. The order to
cease fire, however, was so much delayed, that for
a couple of hours some fighting took place in Jutland, but by the end of the day German troops had
already reached the Skaw.

In a special declaration from the German Commander-in-Chief, General von Kaupisch, the
following promises were given to the Danish
people:

That Germany would not create for herself in
Denmark bases for the struggle against
England;
The Danish army and fleet were to be main-
tained;
The Danish people's freedom would be fully
respected and the country's independence fully
guaranteed.

THE 'MODEL PROTECTORATE'. The idea, as one of
the higher German representatives declared, was
that Denmark should be treated as a 'Model
Protectorate'. The King and Government were
to continue their functions as usual, and the only
restrictions imposed were to be those dictated by
military necessity. The Germans, in fact, tried to
keep up a surface appearance of complete nor-

mality in Denmark. The purpose was two-fold:
first they wanted to prevent the establishment of
any semblance of unity between Norway and Denmark, and secondly Hitler, at the time when he
was preparing his campaigns against the Low
Countries and France, wanted to hold out the
treatment accorded to Denmark as a lure to other
countries in the hope that these might be brought
to capitulate.

Some divergences may, however, have existed
between the various schools of political thought in
Germany, for during the summer of 1940 one
group at any rate tried to support the Danish Nazi
leader, Frits Clausen, whom they wished to see
installed as the Danish quisling. By the end of
November this idea was definitely abandoned, and
it is noteworthy that neither at that time, nor later,
did the Germans find a quisling for Denmark.

However, in the new Danish Foreign Minister,
Erik Scavenius, Berlin found a man who, within
certain limits, was willing to accept the inevitable
consequences of the occupation, and for three
years, first as Foreign Minister and later also as
Prime Minister, he did everything possible to keep
the reins of Government in Danish hands—even
to the extent of acceding to German demands.
When, however, the Germans at last required the
Danish authorities to introduce martial law to stop
the resistance of the Danish people, he refused to
do this and resigned his office.

GERMAN PERFIDY. As might have been expected,
the Germans from the outset of the occupation
started breaking the promises they had made in

their declaration of April 9, 1940, for in the same summer they started to build fortifications, especially in Jutland and on the island of Bornholm, and set to work on the construction of several new aerodromes, so that they were able to use Denmark as a base in their struggle against Britain. The aerodrome at Aalborg, which maintained a connexion with Norway, was actually the largest in northern Europe. Later on in the war, when Germany was forced into the defensive, the fortifications were greatly extended so that the western wall was completed also in the north. In February 1941, the Germans demanded the handing over of six motor torpedo-boats belonging to the Danish navy, and later on the equipment and arms of the Danish army were requisitioned. Danish troops were expelled from Jutland in 1943, and their barracks were taken over by the *Wehrmacht*; shortly after these events the whole Danish army was disarmed.

The first few months of the occupation soon proved that, as regards the third promise made by the Germans, that they would not interfere in the internal affairs of the country, there was no intention of keeping their word. Several leading politicians were forced to resign, foremost among them Mr Christmas Möller, leader of the Conservative Party and Minister of Trade, who eventually escaped to England and became the leader of the Free Danish Movement. The Germans also ordered dismissals and imposed restrictions upon journalists, authors and public speakers; and even at this early stage they tried, though without success, to introduce German judicial procedure against those

who offended them. The most flagrant breach of
Danish laws took place in June 1941, immediately
after Hitler's attack on Russia, when the Danish
Government was forced to arrest all Communists,
dissolve the Communist Party and recall the Danish
Minister from Moscow. Under pressure from
Germany Denmark signed the Anti-Comintern
Pact in April 1941. The Germans, however, had
less success in raising a corps of 'volunteers' to
fight on the Russian front. The fact that the Germans kept the size of this corps a military secret
can be taken as an indication that it was very
small.

ATTITUDE OF THE DANISH GOVERNMENT. Although
these actions contravened Danish constitutional
law, the Government, headed by the old Social
Democratic leader, Thorvald Stauning, who had
been Prime Minister for more than ten consecutive years, and Erik Scavenius, had the support of
the majority of the Danish Parliament. Stauning
and Scavenius, unlike many of the Danish people,
both believed that Germany would win the war,
and, although both of them were anti-Nazi in their
outlook, they were convinced that a new Europe
would be formed with Germany as the natural
leader. Their principal ideas were to prevent Denmark from becoming a theatre of war, to maintain
Danish administration and forms of justice, and
to keep the country's production machinery intact.
To do these things they were prepared to go a long
way towards meeting German demands, but it can
be said that even at that time they had made up
their minds that certain limits would not be ex-

ceeded; for instance, conscription of Danish citizens to take part in the war, the introduction of the Nuremberg anti-Jewish legislation and imposition of the German penal code could not be tolerated in Denmark. The Foreign Minister was able to carry through his programme of collaboration only under considerable and ever-growing resistance from Parliament, and some of the most important steps he wished to take were actually prevented by the action of the King and Parliament. Of these measures the most noteworthy, put forward in July–August 1940, were a suggested customs and monetary union between Germany and Denmark, and an attempted political union under which Danes and Germans would have had equal rights of citizenship in both countries.

GERMAN LOSSES AND GAINS. For the first two years of the occupation, Erik Scavenius actually succeeded in obtaining the advantages for which he was working. Danish administration continued to function much as usual, even though the Germans introduced a German supervised censorship of press and radio, and, moreover, the Germans were not able to commandeer as much as they would have liked in the way of food supplies. They had to conclude a new agreement for deliveries from Denmark every six months, and available figures show that Danish producers succeeded to a considerable extent in cutting down supplies to the Reich. For instance, before the war, Denmark exported 150,000 tons of butter a year, of which 35,000 tons went to Germany, but, after the occupation, exports of butter to the Reich declined to

30,000 tons a year. Since Denmark used to draw
the bulk of her foodstuffs for livestock from the
western world and her source of supply was cut
off by the German occupation, the animal population had immediately to be cut down. The reduction, however, was not as drastic as might have
been expected, for Danish farmers, somehow or
other, managed to produce substitute feed. The
following table shows the position in 1943 compared with 1938:

	%			%	
Milk	78	of 1938	Horses	106	of 1938
Butter	66	,,	Horned cattle	99	,,
Beef and veal	68	,,	Cows	90	,,
Pork	60	,,	Pigs	71	,,
Eggs	28	,,	Fowls	54	,,

The comparatively great decline in butter production, compared with the decline in the number
of cows, is due to the fact that Danish farmers did
all they could to preserve their dairy herds intact,
even though their yield was bound to decline owing
to poverty of diet. When the war is over, proper
feeding will soon bring them back to their former
efficiency.

Generally speaking, industrial output was also
maintained.

Where Scavenius did lose, however, was in the
matter of German interference with the moral and
judicial life of the Danish people.

On their side, the Germans gained, in addition
to the use of the country as a base against Britain
and as transit territory to Norway, as much agricultural produce and fish as they wanted after the
needs of the Danish population had been met.

They also had a contribution from Danish industry, which may not have amounted quantitatively to much, but which still had a certain value as the work was done in factories undisturbed by Allied bombing. Moreover, the Germans were able to take advantage of certain specialized services, such as those of expert diesel-engine constructors and others. Finally, they were able to force a number of Danish workers to go to Germany by creating artificial unemployment, to achieve which they cut down vital supplies of raw materials and coal to Denmark.

Needless to say none of the Danish 'exports' to Germany were paid for by the Germans. They introduced instead a system under which all payments to Danish suppliers were made by the Danish National Bank, which had to enter all the amounts on the so-called 'clearing account' to be settled at some unspecified date. The debt on this clearing account, together with the costs of the occupation, amounted by the end of 1943 to about 5,000,000,000 Kroner (£250,000,000)—which may be compared with a total expenditure before the war of 500,000,000 Kroner per annum (£25,000,000).

RESISTANCE GROUPS. Erik Scavenius was conducting his policy in face of the growing suspicion of the population. From the beginning of the occupation there had been hatred of the Germans, who, in their new guise as Nazis, only too well reminded the Danes of old imperialist Germany, which, in 1864, had robbed them of South Jutland. Part of this loss had been made good after the

Allied victory of 1918, but resentment still lived
on in a population which alone among the
northern countries had suffered from German expansion. Under the new aggression this hatred
at first found expression only vaguely in cold-
shouldering and ridiculing the invaders. But the
fall of France, two months after the German
occupation of Denmark, showed the Danes that
the war would be a long one, and that the participation in it of occupied countries would be needed.
During the Battle of Britain, when Great Britain
alone was facing the enemy, resistance started to
crystallize in the formation of resistance groups—
although eighteen gloomy months were destined
to pass before the organizations were ready to do
their work in real earnest. By the summer of 1942,
however, sabotage workers were proving that they
were fully capable of carrying out the policy of
destruction long advocated by the illegal press.
They did it, indeed, to such good effect that the
Germans forced the Prime Minister, Vilhelm Buhl,
who had succeeded Stauning to this office on the
death of the latter in May 1942, to issue a warning
to the people that Danish justice would be im-
perilled if sabotage continued. This called for a
reply, and it was forthcoming from London. Four
days later, Mr Christmas Möller, leader of the Free
Danes, came to the microphone and told the Danes
that sabotage must go on. And it continued.

**GERMAN DEMANDS FOR A CHANGE OF GOVERN-
MENT.** In November 1942 the first major crisis
occurred. The Germans realized that their policy
had failed in Denmark; after dismissing their

own military and civil authorities, they demanded
that a new Government, with Erik Scavenius as
Prime Minister, should be installed. Contrary to all
expectations, this German-appointed Cabinet was
received comparatively calmly by the population,
partly because it included a number of good Danes
(amongst them several who were not politicians),
and partly because everybody in the country, including Scavenius, knew that this was the last
Danish Government that could be formed under
the occupation.

Scavenius was aware that he was confined within
very narrow limits and that he might not transgress
them. His Government, strangely enough, had a
longer life than anyone would have imagined
possible, and this was mainly due to the fact that
Dr Werner Best, the newly appointed German
plenipotentiary, behaved very differently from
what was expected from a high-ranking S.S. man.
For seven to eight months he made no major
demands on Denmark. As the climax of the war
seemed to approach, however, the German political representative ceased to be the only pebble
on the beach—the army insisted on taking a hand.
A German military Commander-in-Chief could
hardly be expected to close his eyes to the
growing number of acts of sabotage and the
increasing reluctance of the population to aid in
the construction of fortifications. During July and
August 1943 tension had grown so great that an
explosion was bound to follow.

THE ILLEGAL PRESS. As already mentioned, sabotage, since the summer of 1942, had assumed very

serious proportions, from the German point of view. The way had been prepared by the illegal press, which, from rather dull beginnings, had progressed into a really excellent news service, publishing rather more than half a million copies of printed or duplicated papers each month. Some of the Danish illegal papers, most of which are monthly, give their readers up to 16 pages of news and photographs in each issue, and some of the pictures are of first-rate interest. There were, for instance, the photographs of American airmen, shot down over Denmark, being conducted on a sight-seeing tour of Copenhagen before being brought to safety in Sweden. The illegal papers have representatives in all Government departments and all important organizations, who provide information, thus enabling leader writers to give guidance to the population. These illegal papers, of which the biggest has a circulation of 100,000 copies, are produced in some twenty-five printing shops and duplicating offices all over the country, thus guaranteeing quick and equal distribution.

METHODS OF RESISTANCE.   From the outset of their existence the illegal papers consistently advocated the most active forms of resistance.   Naturally enough the results that most caught the eye of the outside world were the acts of sabotage, but other sorts of resistance were developing as well.   First, the administration, which, with very few exceptions, worked all along for Danish interests under cover of an ostensible collaboration, did what was possible to oppose the Germans.   Then there was the more or less passive resistance of the mass

of the people: this showed itself in 'go slow' movements and in sabotage of the type which only
comes to light when, for instance, cars purchased
by the German army broke down hopelessly just
as they arrived at the eastern front. Later on,
however, when the sabotage campaign reached its
height, the workers became more openly engaged
and organized strikes.

When sabotage was at its worst, from the German point of view, there were about 300 major
cases in the course of a single month, and in order
to provide a picture of the sort of damage that was
done, one week can be quoted, that beginning on
May 2, 1944:

May 2. The transformer station at Copenhagen
free port was wrecked. The effects of this was that
all industrial plants in the free port area, where
several of the most important industries are located,
were put out of action for four weeks. The exception to this was the important machine-gun factory
Industrisyndikatet, which has its own power station,
and was, therefore, made the object of a special
attack six days later, on May 8.

May 3. The Globe factory at Glostrup, working
100 % for the Germans, was the scene of something resembling a real partisan battle, for it was
taken by patriots after a frontal assault, and
destroyed.

May 5. The important Scaniadam garage, engaged on repairs for the Germans, was blown up
and fourteen German vehicles destroyed in the
process. The P. Sörensen machine factory, working
to capacity for the Germans, was put out of action.

May 6. The big multiple entertainments building,

Kilden at Aalborg, which had been taken over for the use of the Germans, was destroyed. The aerodrome at Klövermarksvej, formerly belonging to the Danish army, now taken over by the German Luftwaffe, was the scene of one of the biggest and most daring sabotage coups during the whole course of the war. All the workshops and a hangar were totally destroyed.

May 8. One of the most important workshops, turning out world-famous diesel engines, in the Burmeister and Wain shipbuilding yards, was destroyed.

To complete the picture of what sabotage meant in the daily life of the Danish people, it should be added that the Nazi counter-sabotage corps, as a reply to this excellent week of destruction, blew up five of the big department stores in Copenhagen in one night.

Most of the saboteurs are young Danes, who are drawn from all classes of the population, and who have been keeping to a skilfully prepared plan, synchronizing their sabotage with the Allied bomber offensive in other countries. A close study of the nature of the sabotage shows that when the bombers are out to hit shipbuilding yards and ports, the saboteurs in Denmark aim at the same time at the same targets.

A special technique was worked out for what might be called 'phoney' sabotage. On one occasion, for instance, the stationmaster at Copenhagen's principal station received a telephone call saying that bombs had been placed in the station area. The people had to be hurried from the station and no trains were able to enter or leave it for several hours, during which an intensive search was made for non-existent bombs. This, of course, upset the railway time-table for the day. On eleven consecutive days the great shipbuilding firm of Burmeister and Wain received similar anonymous telephone calls, and on each occasion all the 10,000 workers insisted on leaving. The only way in which the Germans could counter this type of sabotage was to close down all public telephone kiosks.

STRIKES. Following some greater acts of sabotage in Esbjerg in August 1943, the Germans reacted with very severe counter-measures, to which the citizens of that most important harbour town, which houses the largest German garrison in Denmark, replied by coming out in a general strike in which one and all joined, not only workers, but shop-keepers, police, municipal authorities, clerks and so on. This strike actually paralysed the life of the city, and the Germans had to give in and repeal their punitive measures. Encouraged by the good results achieved at Esbjerg, other provincial towns, Aalborg and Odense, followed suit. In Odense the Germans were actually obliged to withdraw their soldiers from the streets for a couple of days in order to calm the population. At the end of the month Dr Best flew to Berlin to get new orders. He came back with an ultimatum demanding that the Danish Government should introduce a state of emergency throughout the whole country, pro-hibit public gatherings and strikes, enforce a curfew between 8.30 p.m. and 5 a.m., set up Danish summary courts of justice and introduce death sentences for sabotage, attacks on German army personnel and the possession of firearms and explosives. Furthermore, there were special demands upon the town of Odense, where there had been attacks on German soldiers including a fatality, and where the Germans wished to take hostages until the culprits had been surrendered.

RESIGNATION OF THE DANISH GOVERNMENT. The ultimatum was delivered to the Government on August 28, and the answer had to be given at 4 p.m. on the same day. There were consultations not only with as many Members of Parliament as were available but also with representatives of important organizations, such as the trade unions, and there was certainly no doubt about the feelings of the population as they were then expressed. When the Cabinet met the King there was no wavering and the decision to reject the ultimatum was unanimous. The decision was immediately followed by the resignation of the Government, and the King, shaking hands with each in turn, thanked them for their unanimity in that serious hour, saying that it was of the utmost importance both internally and externally that all should be united.

CHAPTER VI

DENMARK UNDER THE GERMANS (2)

A SECOND INVASION. In the night between Saturday, August 28, and Sunday, August 29, 1943, the Germans invaded Denmark for the second time. Considerable forces of troops had been gathered outside Copenhagen and other important places, and the small Danish garrisons were soon overwhelmed. The Germans, however, were robbed of at least one important prize. The chief of the Danish navy sent out orders that the ships were to try to escape to Sweden, and if they were unable to do so, to scuttle themselves. Fourteen ships, of various sizes, actually escaped with their crews to Swedish ports, and most of the rest were scuttled.

The Germans immediately introduced martial law, and it lasted for thirty-nine days. Yet the emergency regulations had to be lifted at the end of the period without any signs of a Danish retreat having been observed. The King, who for the whole period of the occupation had been the rallying point for the people, now considered himself a prisoner of the Germans, and neither Government nor Parliament functioned.

FAILURE OF DANISH NAZI PARTY. Dr Best tried in vain to find any Danes who would form a sort of Government so as to preserve an outward semblance of collaboration with the Germans. But, when the Germans had most need of its services, the ignominious Danish Nazi Party had virtually ceased to exist. This was certainly not because the Germans did not try to strengthen it. The 'leader', Frits Clausen, who disappeared for good at the beginning of March 1943, had been given all the support he needed to form a strong Nazi Party—had there been any chance of achieving such a thing in Denmark. He was given full economic and political help, but the Danish people soon proved that they were antipathetic to Nazism. The proof came in March 1943, when Clausen's party, the only political group allowed to carry on an election campaign, received only 2 % of the votes cast in a record poll at the general election. The Nazis, moreover, had to cease publication of two out of their three papers, and the only survivor had, at the time of writing, a circulation of which any illegal newspaper would have been ashamed. In fact, the Nazi Party in Denmark, which was constructed on the *Führerprinzip*, now has no Führer, and its tattered remnants are governed by a body of three nonentities.

JEWISH PERSECUTION. As the Germans could not find any support for the Nazis and there was no Danish quisling with whom they could work, and as they could not stop sabotage, they followed their usual practice in such circumstances and started a persecution of the Jews. Denmark and Norway are probably the two European countries in which the Jewish question has played the smallest role. It is related that soon after the occupation began a high German official talking to the King asked him how it was that there did not seem to be a Jewish problem in Denmark. The King replied: 'Well, you see, it is because we Danes do not feel our-selves inferior to the Jews.' The Danish patriotic front made what was probably its greatest humani-tarian effort during the occupation in organizing the mass escape of the Jews to Sweden—7000 went in a few weeks. The Germans were able to capture only about a thousand Jews and Communists. These were deported to Germany, where they were sent to concentration camps. The Jews who escaped to Sweden were later on followed by a similar number of Danish patriots, who, in order to evade the Gestapo, were forced to leave Denmark.

The persecution of the Jews did not, of course, stop Danish resistance, and the Germans had to try and find other means to put an end to the sabotage activities. One method was the obvious one of shooting, deporting or imprisoning the few patriots on whom they could lay hands, but, as the Danish police refused to assist them in any way, these were indeed only a few. The second method was to try to turn the mass of the Danish people against the saboteurs and other illegal workers. This they did by making use of a special corps of Danish supporters established under the name 'Schalburg Corps', called thus after a Danish Nazi volunteer who had died on the eastern front. The members of this corps were ordered to commit sabotage against objectives of purely Danish interest, and, at the same time, they were sent out in all sorts of disguises to try and discover traces of the illegal organizations. In order to preserve their organiza-tions inviolate, the patriots found it necessary to liquidate some of the most notorious denouncers; trusted members of the Schalburg Corps were then ordered by the Germans to murder a number of prominent Danish citizens, including Pastor Kaj Munk, a well-known Danish playwright. There were also a number of attempted murders of political leaders.

DANISH COUNCIL OF FREEDOM. In spite of numerous executions and arrests by the thousand (in the course of one year fifty patriots were executed and more than 100 murdered by the Gestapo or their henchmen of the Schalburg Corps, etc.), the Germans never succeeded in finding their way to the nerve centres of the Freedom Movement. These were represented by the Danish Council of Freedom, which established itself on Danish Constitution Day, June, 5 1943. At first not much attention was paid to this body, but it soon proved to be a very efficient group under the direction of people some of whom were forced to live underground, while others were able to carry on their normal existence without arousing the suspicions of the Germans. Soon the Freedom Council attracted to itself most of the groups who were working separately against the Germans, and it announced that its aim was to co-ordinate 'representatives of all Danish movements which, in agreement with the will of the people, desire actively to combat the German occupying Power until Denmark is again a free and independent country'.

The Freedom Council rapidly began to influence not only the activists but also the Danish illegal press, and later on, when it became necessary, it organized the escape service to Sweden, which up to March 1943 conducted approximately 1000 people per month across the Sound. Representing in the first place about 50 % of the total active front, it later extended its scope to include a number of independent resistance groups, who became loosely associated with it. In the autumn the members of the Council were even able to announce that they had in their midst a representative of the Danish Council in London. Although physically separated by the expanse of the North Sea, these two bodies have to-day succeeded in establishing a close co-operation.

BEFORE AND AFTER D-DAY. When the invasion of Europe approached, the Council of Freedom directed sabotage acts against the sixteen really important Danish factories working for the German war machine, producing parts for aeroplanes and tanks, and making anti-aircraft weapons. The Danes had actually been so efficient in their destruction campaign against Danish production machinery that for eighteen months the R.A.F. had not been obliged to carry out a single attack on a Danish plant. When D-Day arrived no fewer than eleven of the sixteen major factories were already out of order, and during the first weeks of June the remaining five were dealt with. The biggest of these was the only important arms factory in Denmark, The Rifle Syndicate, situated in the strongly guarded Free Port of Copenhagen. On 22 June what must be described as a real partisan attack was made upon this enterprise. Armoured cars, manned by 125 patriots, stormed

the factory and office buildings in broad daylight
at 6 p.m. The sabotage guards were quickly over-
powered and fifteen T.N.T. bombs planted all over
the premises, but not until a number of 20 mm.
automatic guns, mounted on carriages, many
machine guns and sufficient ammunition to stock
the arsenals of the patriots for some time to come
had been carried off. The whole factory was completely demolished, and it will not produce another
gun for the duration of this war. This was the
climax of the patriots' sabotage campaign against
industrial plants. From then on they transferred
their activities to communication lines in Jutland,
so as to co-ordinate their efforts with those made
by the underground workers in other occupied
countries.

Before all this happened the Germans tried to
strike with all their might so as to quench the
resistance of the Danish people. In one week
sixteen patriots were executed, of whom one-half
came from a tiny village in Jutland, where every
tenth person was put to death. Furthermore, the
Germans introduced a curfew in Copenhagen and
summary courts of justice were set up all over
Zealand and, in order to provoke public feeling,
the Schalburg Corps of traitors was sent out into
the streets to create as many incidents and accidents
as possible.

DANISH REPLY TO THE CURFEW. It was actually
the introduction of the curfew at the early hour
of 8 p.m. in the height of summer that roused
the opposition of the people. The 10,000 workers
in the famous shipbuilding yards of Burmeister

and Wain, in Copenhagen, went on strike and even sent a challenging letter to the German plenipotentiary, Dr Best, stating that it was more important to them to get the vegetables from their allotments outside the city than to serve the German war industry. The following day the workers of most of the factories in Copenhagen followed suit, and in the evenings the citizens had the effrontery to flout the curfew and walk out in the streets, while the Freedom Council even arranged a firework display before the Gestapo headquarters in the centre of the city, in mockery of the flying bombs on England. On this occasion leaflets were also distributed, bearing a greeting which the Allied High Command had sent to the Danish saboteurs.

The Germans were furious and promptly sent out soldiers, Gestapo men and members of the Schalburg Corps into the streets to fire indiscriminately upon the crowds. After a week of such attempts at intimidation the whole population of Copenhagen had joined the strike. All Ministries, factories, shops and offices closed, telegraph and telephone services ceased to work, and in fact the whole life of the capital was paralysed. Night after night the people poured into the streets and lit bonfires—as many as 1000 were observed in a single night—and the Germans went on sending firing squads all over the town. These were hindered by great barricades erected across the streets to the height of second floor windows. In one street Germans could be heard shouting: 'Shut all windows, or we fire!' and the reply from a Dane came two minutes later: 'Open all windows quickly—a factory is about to be blown up!' The few Danish warehouse owners who had worked willingly for the Germans had their property destroyed during these days of strike.

The Germans completely lost all hold on the population—even low-flying aircraft machine-gunning the streets failed to disperse the crowds. Ninety-four Copenhageners were killed by German bullets in a week. The food situation became bad, but there were still no signs of giving in. The Germans were at a loss to know how to deal with the situation. First they tried to be placatory by cutting down the number of hours of the curfew, but the strike simply went on. Then Dr Best decided to oppose steel with steel. If food was scarce—well, he would see to it that the people of Copenhagen got no food at all. He closed down the public services of water, gas and electricity and stopped all transport from entering the capital. He also announced that anyone trying to leave Copenhagen would be shot. A wonderful community spirit was seen during these days. All the food left was fairly divided amongst the citizens, without regard to payment. Street worked with neighbouring street by sending out patrols in the vicinity to get what supplies could be obtained from nearby farms. And all the time the spirit of resistance grew.

On Sunday, July 2, the Germans, after consultation with the leading Danish politicians, decided to return to conciliatory methods. As previously they had shortened the curfew hours, they now reopened water, gas and electricity services. The radio, which had been silent for 48 hours, sent out proclamations from the chiefs of the administrative depart-

ments and representatives of the political parties
asking the people to go back to work.

SUCCESS OF THE GENERAL STRIKE. The strike had
started spontaneously, but now Denmark's Underground Freedom Council decided to take the lead.
The appeal to return to work put out by the
authorities was ignored. The Freedom Council on
the following day, Monday, July 3, issued a procla-
mation to the people of Copenhagen asking them
to continue the strike until the Germans had given
in on the following points:

(1) The Schalburg Corps of Danish traitors to
be removed from the streets of Copenhagen, and
to be either deported or interned.

(2) The curfew to be abolished.

(3) All public services and traffic to be restored
to normal.

(4) The Germans to promise that no reprisals
would be taken.

Two things now happened which led to the complete defeat of Dr Best. The strike spread from
Copenhagen to twenty-two provincial towns and
furthermore to five of the great co-operative dairies
which supplied Germany with all the dairy products
she received from Denmark. Secondly, Dr Walter,
a high official from Berlin, arrived in Copenhagen
in order to settle the trouble—which had caused
great concern in Germany. In these circumstances
Dr Best had to give in on all four points, and the
following day, Tuesday, July 4, work was resumed
in Denmark.

The People's Strike in Copenhagen was the first
instance of a capital city rising unarmed against the

German oppressors. In its scope it was limited; there was no idea at that time of throwing out the Germans, because the leaders of the resistance knew that they had to await the orders of the Allied High Command. Nevertheless, definite aims were in view, and these were attained. With absolute confidence the Danish people await the day on which the signal heralding the final reckoning will be given.

Shortly after this victory over the German occupying Power, the Danish underground movement succeeded in reconnecting the tie with Russia which had been broken after the German attack on the Soviet Union in 1941. Representatives of the Free Danes abroad had long ago established contact with the representatives of the Soviet Union to assure them that the severing of diplomatic relations between Denmark and themselves had taken place against the will of the Danish people and only on orders from Germany. The underground Freedom Council now came forward with the suggestion that a man representing the patriotic home front should be sent to Russia as representative of Fighting Denmark both at home and abroad. Moscow quickly replied that it was willing to accept a representative coming from Denmark and would give him diplomatic rank. In August 1944, Dr Thomas Dössing, chief of the Danish Library Commission, was received in Moscow.

POST-LIBERATION PLANS OF THE FREEDOM COUNCIL. For the time being, the Freedom Council, besides telling people what they must do if there is an invasion by the Allies and training them for this purpose, has found time to outline programmes for the period immediately following the liberation of Denmark. Although in fighting the Germans its members have had to offend against the law, they are nevertheless making their plans for the future in strict accordance with those laws which circumstances now compel them to violate. The programme for the future conforms completely to the traditional Danish code of justice; there is no suggestion of the 'eye for an eye and tooth for a tooth' mentality. Even now the Council repudiates such acts of violence as that done in the Mokka Café, Copenhagen, which did no material damage to the German war effort other than killing and wounding a few individual members of the *Wehrmacht*, and even killed and injured some Danish citizens. Where the struggle against the occupying Power demands the exemplary punishment of an individual, such punishment must be inflicted upon the person responsible for a specific crime, and not imposed indiscriminately.

So soon as the occupation troops leave Denmark, the Council declares that Parliament should immediately be summoned and the King should appoint a Government. It is not very likely that the Freedom Council and the activists connected with them would be willing to accept the Cabinet proposed by the old politicians, as reported in April 1944 in the Swedish press. As Mr Christmas Möller has pointed out in London, the new Government should certainly include representatives of the abolished Communist Party and of the activists' national party, *Dansk Samling*, as well as of the Freedom Council itself. The Freedom Council also proposes that all Nazi elements should be imprisoned, Nazi organizations dissolved, and civil servants and others who have been guilty of or accessory to the violation of Danish principles of justice during the occupation, or who have derived personal gain from it, should be held responsible for their actions. It further declares that all German-dictated laws should be abolished as soon as possible, and all those put in prison for patriotic deeds or words immediately released.

In the view of the resistance leaders the Government to be appointed should provide for parliamentary elections, as the Parliament elected in March 1943 does not lawfully fulfil the requirements of democratic parliamentary representation. It is thought that not until the new Parliament has been elected and a Government based on this election formed, will it be possible to decide what is to be done with war criminals. Many problems will have to be solved: for instance, is it punishable to have been a Nazi? The Freedom Council does not think so, and does not agree to placing any prohibition on the Party, but of course those Nazis who have allowed themselves to be bought as traitors will have to be brought to book in accordance with new laws which will have to take effect retrospectively. This represents the only point of departure from the Danish penal code, but it has been found a necessary one.

ALLIED OCCUPATION OF DANISH TERRITORIES. One year after the occupation of Denmark, President Roosevelt, through his Secretary for Foreign Affairs, Mr Cordell Hull, concluded an agreement

with the Danish Minister in Washington, Mr
Henrik Kauffmann, concerning Greenland, under
which the United States undertook temporarily the
protection of that territory. This agreement, which
has proved very useful to both parties, provides
that after the war Greenland will be returned to
the sovereign jurisdiction of Denmark. Greenland
has provided extremely useful naval and air bases
for the United Nations, and, on the other hand,
the native population was assured of the supplies
which used to be drawn exclusively from Denmark.

Iceland, which shared the crown of Denmark,
was occupied by the British Navy on May 10, 1940,
and in July 1941 America took over the protection
of Iceland from Britain, having first co-operated
there with the latter. On June 17, 1944, Iceland,
following a plebiscite, proclaimed a republic and
dissolved its connexion with the Danish crown.

The small Faeroe Islands were occupied by
British forces on April 10, 1940, solely as a war-
time measure.

DANES IN BRITAIN.   On the day of the occupation
of Denmark about half a million tons of Danish
merchant shipping, together with some 4000
Danish sailors, went to British or Allied ports,
where they have since been serving, both in
bringing in supplies and in carrying the forces
of invading armies to Africa and to Europe.
A small unit of minesweepers manned by Danes
is operating with the Royal Navy. Some few
hundreds of young Danes who were living outside
Denmark or who had succeeded in escaping thence

to Britain joined the army, navy or air force as volunteers.

Very shortly after the invasion of Denmark the Free Danish Movement was formed in Great Britain and Northern Ireland, with Mr Kröyer-Kielberg as President, and, in May 1942, the former leader of the Conservative Party, Mr Christmas Möller, dispossessed of all his offices by the Germans, arrived in England. He became Chairman of the Danish Council, which was responsible for the great work of furthering and inspiring the resistance movement both at home and abroad. The Danish Minister in Great Britain, Count Reventlow, who broke with the Danish Government in December 1941, then joined the movement as its Honorary President.

Immediately before the invasion of the Continent it was declared officially, that during the period of liberation, Denmark would be treated as an Ally.

APPENDIX

CENTRAL GOVERNMENT. Denmark is a democratic monarchy. The constitution lays it down that legislative authority is vested jointly in the Crown and Parliament. Executive power rests with the Crown, while the administration of justice is exercised by the courts. The established Church is the Evangelical Lutheran Church, and to it the King must belong. Constitutionally, the King can do no wrong, and he exercises his authority through the Ministers appointed by himself to be responsible for the government of the country. The Ministers may be impeached by the King or the Lower House in matters relating to the discharge of their official duties, such cases being tried before the High Court of the Realm. Without Parliament's consent the King cannot declare war or conclude peace, enter into or denounce alliances or commercial treaties, cede any part of the country, or enter into any obligation which alters the constitutional status of the country.

The Danish Parliament (*Rigsdag*) consists of the *Folketing* (the Lower House) and the *Landsting* (Upper House), the former having 149 and the latter seventy-six members. There are four main political parties represented in Parliament, namely, the Conservative, the Social Democrats (the most powerful), the Liberal Lefts,[1] who in the main

---

[1] The 'Left' in Danish politics applies to Liberals. The Social Democrats are the Socialist Party.

represent the interests of the farmers, and the
Radical Lefts, chiefly supporting the interests of the
small farmers and smallholders. The Communist
and Nazi Parties are both small in numbers. At
the April 1939 elections the former received 40,893
and the latter 31,032 votes, each securing three
seats in the Lower House.

All men and women of Danish nationality (women
received the franchise in 1915) above the age of 25
possess voting rights (with certain exceptions in
the case, for instance, of persons convicted of 'dis-
honourable offences', or undischarged bankrupts,
etc.). *Folketing* members are elected for four-
year periods. To vote in the *Landsting* elections
men and women alike must have attained the age
of 35 and must be permanent residents in the
Landsting constituency concerned.

LOCAL GOVERNMENT. Denmark consists of twenty-
two *Amter* (counties), not including the Faeroe
Islands. The chief state official of the *Amt* is the
Amtmand (Prefect). The other important officials
are the *Amtslaege* or *Kredeslaege* (Medical Officer
of Health) and the *Amtsvejinspektör* (County Sur-
veyor of Roads).

There are eighty-eight towns, each constituting
a municipality. The highest permanent official is
the *Borgmester* or *Formand*. He is head of the
municipal services. The permanent Secretary of
the Council is called the *Raadmand*, who deals
especially with financial matters. He will not be
found in smaller towns.

The *Stadsingeniör* (Borough Engineer) is head
of all technical services, and deals with matters

relating to water supply, sewage, fire service, construction and maintenance of roads and bridges, town planning, building regulations, etc. The *Kommunelaege* is the Medical Officer of Health. The *Arbejdsanvisningskontor* is the Labour Exchange, and this is headed by a local Manager.

Socialinspektören are the Poor Relief Officer and Public Assistance Officer, and the *Rationeringsudvalg* is the local Supply Committee. The *Priskontrollör* is the local Price Controller. The *Kaemner* is the Collector of Local Taxes and the Town Accountant.

In larger towns the same set-up will be found, but on a correspondingly larger scale. In Copenhagen, for instance, there is an *Overpraesident* (Chief State Official), one *Overborgmester* and five *Borgmestre*, and there are also five *Raadmaend*. The Chief of Police is the *Politidirektör*, while he is called the *Politimester* in the provinces.

There are 1292 rural districts. The Chairman of the Council is the *Sogneraadsformand*. The permanent Secretary of the Council is the *Sogneraadssekretaer*, whose duties correspond to those of the *Raadmand* in the towns. The *Sogneraadskasserer* is the Tax Collector and Accountant, corresponding to the *Kaemner* in the towns. The *Sognefoged* is the Parish Sheriff, who is concerned with various police and fire service duties.

Denmark is divided up into nine *Stifter* (dioceses), consisting of ninety-three *Provstier* (deaneries) and 1290 *Pastorater* (parishes).

Headmasters of schools are called *Skolebestyrer* or *Overlaerer*, except in Grammar Schools where

they are called *Rektors*. Schoolmasters generally
are called *Laerer* and schoolmistresses *Laererinde*.

CURRENCY, WEIGHTS AND MEASURES. The currency
is the Danish *Krone*, or Crown, which is divided
into *Öre*, of which there are 100 to the *Krone*.
The par value of the *Krone* was about 18.50 to
the pound sterling.

The metric system of weights and measures
applies in Denmark.

SOCIAL INSURANCE. Denmark's most important
contribution to social legislation, which stands
generally on a very high level, is to be found in
the sphere of social insurance. 'Support for self-
support' is the slogan under which this was evolved.
In Denmark the state organizes and regulates insurance; sometimes it runs the insurance company
itself. A far-reaching reform of the social insurance
laws was passed through Parliament in 1933.

In Denmark everyone has to be insured, including washerwomen and cleaning women—no
wage earner is excluded from this obligation; thus
they are all eligible for benefit if they become
unemployed. Under modern legislation, moreover, all unemployment societies are compelled to
pay into continuation funds so that workers may
continue to receive relief at the end of the period
covered by their ordinary unemployment insurance.

While insurance against unemployment and
accident are limited to workers, sickness and other
kinds of social insurance are open to every citizen.
Health insurance is by law compulsory for every-

one. On reaching the age of 21 every person must join a Sick Benefit Society or the State Sickness Insurance Association. To the sickness insurance is attached an invalidity insurance scheme, which is compulsory for all between the ages of 21 and 60 years. Under this scheme there are extra allowances for the disabled and the blind.

A system of old age pensions is also attached to the sickness insurance, but, although this is given the name 'insurance', it is actually public relief paid entirely by the State and municipality. This pension is available to people on reaching the age of 60, but it is increased if the pensioners wait one, two, or more years before claiming it.

The Danish people were well on their way towards establishing a State in which all who are in need receive care, but the unemployment problem has not yet been fully solved. In the years immediately preceding the war the Government forbade over-time work in industry and commerce, introduced holidays with pay (a fortnight in industry and commerce and a week in agriculture) and subsidized private building enterprises to relieve unemployment.

INDEX

For EU product safety concerns, contact us at Calle de José Abascal, 56–1°,
28003 Madrid, Spain or eugpsr@cambridge.org.

www.ingramcontent.com/pod-product-compliance
Ingram Content Group UK Ltd.
Pitfield, Milton Keynes, MK11 3LW, UK
UKHW012327130625
459647UK00009B/117